Motivation

How to Unleash Your Inner Motivation to Achieve Everything You Have Ever Wanted and Enjoy the Process

By Maya Faro

Copyright Maya Faro©2016

All rights reserved. No part of this publication may be reproduced, stored in a retrieval system, or transmitted, in any form or by any means, electronic, mechanical, photocopying, recording or otherwise, without the prior written permission of the author and the publishers.

The scanning, uploading, and distribution of this book via the Internet, or via any other means, without the permission of the author is illegal and punishable by law. Please purchase only authorized electronic editions, and do not participate in or encourage electronic piracy of copyrighted materials.

All information in this book has been carefully researched and checked for factual accuracy. However, the author and publishers make no warranty, expressed or implied, that the information contained herein is appropriate for every individual, situation or purpose, and assume no responsibility for errors or omission. The reader assumes the risk and full responsibility for all actions, and the author will not be held liable for any loss or damage, whether consequential, incidental, and special or otherwise, that may result from the information presented in this publication.

Contents

Introduction 5

Chapter 1 Negative Habits and Mental Patterns That Destroy Your Motivation 8

    The Self-Love Detox 8

    Negative Self-Talk 9

    Judgment and How It Can Kill Your Motivation 13

Chapter 1 Self-Love Influx: How to Actually Love Yourself to Get and Stay Motivated 18

    Intrinsic vs Extrinsic Motivation 21

    The Self-Love Motivational Boot Camp 23

    How to Forgive Yourself (Stop Dwelling on Failures) 24

    Take Some You-Time 27

    When to Say "No" (Just Say "No") 29

    Embrace Patience and Trust the Process 30

Chapter 2 The Best Mind Body Tools to Get and Stay Motivated . 32

    The Power Hour (Inspired by Tony Robbins) 34

    The Power of Journaling- How to Stay Motivated with Journaling (inspired by Julia Cameron) 35

    How to Use Affirmations to Get and Stay Motivated (how to brainwash yourself) 38

    Mcditation to Stay Motivated? 39

    Your Power Hour- How to Get the Best of It and Stay Motivated Throughout the Day 41

Chapter 3 Your Vision for Life and (Vision Boards) 43

Chapter 4 How to Turn Negative into Positive (How to Deal with Adversity) 52

How to Deal with People Who Question Your Self-Improvements 52
Careful with Toxic People... 53
How to Deal with Self-Sabotage 54
Your Awareness is Your Responsibility 57
Your Hero: How to Get Inspired...57

Conclusion: Be Your Best Self 59
Think about TEAM YOU 59
Prioritize Inspiration (aka Brainwash Yourself) 61
Be Specific and Have Deadlines..61
Do Not Take Crap from Anyone 62
Dream Big. Go Big or Go Home. 63
Don't Get Caught Up In "Realistic". 63
Stay In Shape... 63
Keep High Standards for Yourself. 64

Final Words... 66

Introduction

On my 25th birthday, everything was going right. A total catch, I was living in New York City at the time, everyone, even my hot (*really* hot) boyfriend told me every girl should be envious of how on-point my life was. I was young, pretty, and thin with a blossoming theatrical career to boot; I mean, a force to be reckoned with, right?

Er…yeah, not exactly.

You see, when I looked in the mirror all I could think was, *Where is this "force to be reckoned with"? Where is the flourishing individual that everyone is here to celebrate?* I didn't see her. In fact, all I saw was a lost, scared, afraid-of-what-people-thought-of-her, sheepish girl, who should have had her life *way* more together than she did. Suffice it to say, that low self-esteem ship needed to do a serious 180 and change its course – and do so STAT. Though I wasn't old, I also wasn't' getting any younger. So I broke up with my boyfriend – he was kind of a jerk anyway –moved back to my hometown, became obsessed with self-help and spirituality books, recordings, seminars and learned to better myself -- and my life.

So, here I am! Ready to take it a step further and help you ROCK ON in *your* life, career, fitness goals, and whatever other awesome endeavors in your near (and far) future. But most importantly, I want you to achieve your goals not someone else's goals so that you can achieve happiness and fulfilment in your life. As humans, we have every capacity to live proactive, deliberate, self-actualized and fun lives. To show our failures who is boss, to bag up our fears and kick them to the curb. To become the authors of our own stories and rewrite what we don't like – or want to change. To love our heroic and powerful selves.

Chapter 1 Negative Habits and Mental Patterns That Destroy Your Motivation

The Self-Love Detox

This may sound cheesy, but the first step to being successful at just about any aspect of life is to improve your relationship with yourself. To learn (or re-learn) how to love yourself.

To do so, we must first, as the saying goes, go "out with the old". In other words, let's figure out – and then ditch – our pervasive and unhelpful self-talk habits.

Here are some habits, most of which are universal, that are totally ditch-worthy:

Negative Self-Talk

Find it.

If you're anything like me, you may have some *I'm so stupid, I'm ugly, I'm fat, I'm a bad mother/father/husband/wife/baker/candlestick-maker* going on in your head. The first step here is to notice how you talk to yourself.

Notice -- *What am I saying to myself?* Simply, notice.

Note: Do not make judgments or analyze this self-talk – yet. For some reason, we love to beat ourselves up about minor and/or insignificant details such as running five minutes late to a meeting or that "stupid thing" we said to our boss. We editorialize the facts so much so that small details turn into award-winning dramas. Whatever you do, don't go there now.

Throughout the next day or two, make a small list with 2-3 negative things you say to yourself daily. Read it often – and, again, *without judgment*. Simply say, "I say _____ to myself often" – and leave it at that.

Flip it.

The absolute best way to combat negativity in your mind – to wash it away and make room for inspiration and rock-star positive energy – is to reverse the aforementioned negative self-talk with positive affirmations.

Again. Sounds cheesy but, *man*, does it work.

Now, what you want to do here is take your little handy dandy list of negative self-talk (remember that list?) and next to each negative statement, write the positive affirmation next to it. (An affirmation is a statement expressed in the positive voice.)

Let's do an example. Say you constantly tell yourself non-niceties such as "No one will ever hire me because I'm not as smart (successful, determined, etc.) as Juan". First of all, this isn't likely a true statement. Secondly, it will *become true* if you keep pounding that kind of thought into your head, so let's nip it in the bud ASAP.

Now, let's flip it: "No one will hire me because I'm not as smart as Juan" will now become "I am smart and bright, and there are a million people who would love to hire me very soon". (Or something of that nature.)

But what if it's not true, you might be thinking. *I'm not smart or bright or about to be hired…*

The thing about affirmations is that you write them NO MATTER WHAT YOU THINK. It's a tough pill to swallow, but your perception may be off anyway. Trust that there is a world out there in which you are smart, bright and in which a million people would love to hire you very soon.

Another example: "I can't go to the gym because I'm clumsy and overweight". So let's rewrite this story into something more uplifting and, I bet you, more accurate, too.

"I can't go to the gym because I'm clumsy and overweight" could turn into "I am coordinated, agile and excited to go to the gym today".

Again, even if you doubt these affirmations (or this process) with every fiber in your body, continue to write them. Do it anyway. Brainwash yourself! If your up-until-now story is comprised of mostly negative conversations in your head, then, well…you are living and breathing a very negative story. Rewrite this story, my rock-star friend; you *can* and you absolutely *deserve to*.

When it comes to being the hero of your own life and/or the author of your own story, affirmations are such an untapped goldmine; they are worth spending time on. They are a tried-and-true antidote to negative self-talk.

Put some effort in on these, even if it's hard or you don't want to, and write these awesome, positive statements down as frequently as possible – in a notebook, on a napkin, text them to yourself – WHATEVER. Just do them and do them *often*.

Judgment and How It Can Kill Your Motivation

We judge just about everything. Whether it's a meal, a concert, or the service at a restaurant, if we enjoyed it, we use judgment-based terms to describe it and assess it. We call something "good" and if it's not, we say it's "bad" – or a version of either word. "The salad was *great*," we say. Or "It was a really *bad* salad".

Sometimes, and let me emphasize *sometimes*, these sentiments are share-worthy. That being said, value judgments can be very subjective and, thus, not universally true. I mean, what if *I* tried the very salad you disliked and LOVED it?! Was it really a "bad salad" as you said? Or was it simply a salad with more vegetables than you prefer and more along the lines of something *I* would like?

Rearrange your wording and force yourself to take out the value judgment when talking about anything and everything. This will be hard to do, but try it anyway. Here's why:

The consequences are small when we are dealing with a salad. I mean, we won't hurt the salad's feelings or anything – at least let's hope not. With a salad, we are simply assessing the quality of an inanimate, feeling-less object.

But then the line can get a little hairy. In other words, there can be an issue when the ideas behind "good" and "bad" carry over to ourselves, our work, our fitness, our relationships in not-so-flattering – and equally detrimental – ways. This is why taking the value judgments – aka words like "good" and "bad" – out of your vocabulary is so imperative.

For example, let's say you have decided to lose weight by going to the gym five times a week. Day #1 of your regimen you go. Days #2, and #3, you go. And so on. You then tell yourself, "I've been *really good* this week by going to the gym five times". Statements like this start to blur the line between the awesome work you've done by going to the gym five days in one week and the idea that you, yourself, have demonstrated good character, morals, behavior and, in turn, are a person worthy of love and abundance.

Ditch it.

So, now that we know that "the good" and "the bad" are ugly (hehehe...), how do we get rid of these nagging value judgments on ourselves?

The first step is to simply notice when you (and others) use these words to describe something – or in many cases, *everything*. Notice where someone says, "I'm so bad at that" or "You're such a good cook". Again, yes, ultimately you may be a "good cook" but again, start to see if you can't shift this wording in your own mind. Once you start noticing where the words "good" and "bad" pop up – and how often they do! – you can then go in and adjust them.

Let's take the aforementioned gym scenario. You went five times in one week. (Wahoo!!!!) About your efforts, you said, "I was really *good* this week". So, how could we change this to take out as much of the *value* assessment on our gym time and still express that there is a positive outcome?

Here – and bear with me here – we have to get creative and a tiny bit analytical: What do you mean by "I was really good this week"? What does "really good entail"? Instead of the word "good", could you think of a few more adjectives to describe your rockin' gym habit? Try "I was *productive* when it came to my goals this week" or "I *rocked this week* by going to the gym five times".

We are still emphasizing positive (aka "good") things about this week's gym feats, but we are doing so in a way that separates the awesomeness of our actions from the value we place on ourselves as humans. The distinction here is so super important.

A positive self-image is the gateway to some awesome self-love coming your way. So, pay attention to where you can throw in some neutral terminology to describe your efforts. It may seem weird at first, and like it's not helping you. But over time, you will learn that less value judgment in the short term equals incredible self-confidence in the longer term.

Try one more: Say your boss calls you into her office and tells you the report you recently turned in to her had lots of errors and, until they're fixed, the report is pretty much unusable. Cue: tears (you worked really hard on that report) and anger (at your boss) as well as anger at yourself.

"I should have checked it over more thoroughly," you say. "I should have had someone lay a second set of eyes on it". And (drum roll)... *"I did a bad job"*.

But did you?

Let's flip it. Change "I did a bad job" to "My report had several errors (which I am fully capable of correcting)". Voila! Ultimately, yes, it contained errors, but let's lay off the blame on yourself just a bit. Trust me; it will help. In a wonderful way, releasing yourself from "good" and "bad" opens you up to so many more possible lenses through which to see a situation. It forces you to get creative, and, more importantly to remind yourself that you are worthy of more than shallow value judgments. Shallow value judgments are, well, shallow. And we don't need them pecking away at our confidence levels, just when we are aiming to make tons of incredible improvements.

You are enough, and your efforts are fabulous. You are also a beacon of light, so keep going forward and acting as such. Adjusting your wording will help you write or re-write this aspect of your newly changed, more self-actualized story. Deciding to ditch the value judgments gives you longevity in your thinking, flexibility in your perception, and creativity to expand the lenses through which you see the world.

Chapter 1 Self-Love Influx: How to Actually Love Yourself to Get and Stay Motivated

As discussed, here's how it works: you take the reins and release judgment. Thus, you now have a much more "blank canvas" on which to paint your new story. It's a slightly cheesy metaphor, yet incredibly powerful, so hold your horses and don't run off quite yet!

And with a blank canvas, you now have the capacity to welcome in the multitude of wonderful, positive, motivational, inspirational attributes of YOU that already exist and are waiting to be expressed, most specifically, the ability to practice the Queen Bee of positive thinking, abundant self-love.

In the self-help world, everything stems from self-love, which, defined, is exactly like it sounds. And here's the deal with self-love. No matter your past, or present circumstance, you absolutely can have it and practice it. You should, and you will when you get a good taste of it. Self-love is a little addictive – a drug in the best way possible. But what's cool is that you *almost* can't have too much of it. (Self-love is very different than narcissism, by the way.)

So, giving yourself a blank canvas on which to paint the story of your life allows you to start fresh and create the life that *you* want for yourself. *You.* Not your mother, your father, your husband/wife/fastidious grandmother, etc. *You.*

You need a blank canvas for so many reasons, but most of all so you can stop and think, really think about: What do I want out of life? What kind of story do I want to tell about myself, my life?

In other words – and to continue without blank canvas metaphor – what goes at the focal point of the painting (aka: What are the main things I want to happen in my life?) and what is on the periphery (aka: What are details and peripheral events that I want to happen, that are present but just not the focus of everyday life)?

Assessing these questions forces you to do some serious thinking about what is important to you, as well as your motivations. Start to think about the ideas that wake you up in the morning. Coffee, tea, breakfast, a fun workout, the thought of seeing your newborn baby boy? And what do you daydream about? Knitting? Football? Journalism? Becoming a personal trainer? Whatever it is, see it and remember it. Also, what do you picture yourself doing in your dream life?

You can even take a blank piece of notebook paper and write a page describing your ultimate dream life, where you'll wake up, what you're wearing, what activities you'll have going on that day, etc. This is a wonderful exercise, and it has stuck with me for quite some time.

Intrinsic vs Extrinsic Motivation

Your inner-desire and deeper motivations are called *intrinsic motivation*. Intrinsic motivation is the meat-and-potatoes reasoning of why you do what you do. Intrinsic motivation is deep, lasting, and hits you at your very core. It is the mother of all motivation and should be paid special attention to.

Intrinsic motivation includes such factors as what you believe in, what pleases you, what you abhor, and what motivates you deeply. It is the root of sustained desire, which, as we all know, when getting stuff done, is incredibly important to pay attention to.

Conversely, there is *extrinsic motivation*, which is about satisfaction happening more on the exterior, or surface level. Extrinsic motivation includes factors such as appearances, money, or praise from others. Extrinsic motivation can help you stay motivated for a short period of time, but studies have shown that it is intrinsic motivation, sustained desire, that really gets you to your goals.

Let's use the aforementioned example of going to the gym. If you were *intrinsically motivated*, you would go because it feels good to go to the gym, it elevates your mood, and puts you in the driver's seat of your day. *Extrinsic motivations* would include you want to look hot and you want more muscle in your arms. Both can be motivating, but, in my experience, the difference is that intrinsic motivation lines you up for long-term success.

So now that you have a blank canvas and are aware of some of your intrinsic and extrinsic motivations, let's take those and apply them to our metaphor of painting a life picture filled with deliberate self-love and care. You now know what motivates you, both on the inside and out; let's take those motivations, knead them a bit, and lay them out for the base of your story – one immersed in self-love and desire…

The Self-Love Motivational Boot Camp

I am now going to get to the "nitty gritty" on what needs to happen in order to love yourself fully and what tools you can use to access joy, inner-peace, and lasting dedication towards your dreams.

Why? Several reasons, most importantly *why not*? Also, self-love – the practice of caring for and about yourself – is the basis not only of you doing well, but once we satisfy our own needs in terms of care, we are in a much more giving way to care about others.

We all know the image of the mom who does it all for her family. Cooks, cleans, drives kids to soccer practice, packs her husband's suitcase. But what we don't always see on the surface level is how she is perceived to be "perfect" and "caring" – and perhaps she is caring (no one is perfect) – but she very likely feels drained and maybe even a little empty inside. While caring so much for her family, she forgets to care about herself.

We come from a long history of thinking that selflessness is best. "Think of others before you think of yourself", we say. Yes...but also no – at least not in my opinion. Of course, there are some circumstances in which we think or others before ourselves, but the vast majority of giving, thorough, honest and genuine giving comes from a place of feeling satisfied and full ourselves.

So. In a nutshell, here's how to love yourself:

How to Forgive Yourself (Stop Dwelling on Failures)

We already discussed this in short, but let's take it a little further; it is one thing to change the thoughts and words in your head – and our affirmations will help you do so ever so incredibly - but it is quite another to embrace the power behind doing so. For example, you can do the aforementioned affirmations exercises, but you also need to *embrace* the truth behind these affirmations, as well. Practice living out what you affirm.

Say, for example, that your affirmation is, "I give love and love returns to me". (That's a good one to add to your repertoire.) Start noticing situations in your life where this is true. You pick up your kids from school because you love them. You want to see them (maybe not ALL the time – wink, wink), but you absolutely, positively and unconditionally love them. That is an awesome example of you giving love.

Your neighbor drops off a loaf of zucchini bread to your family "just because". That's love – love returning to you, no less. Start noticing these truths and then (drum roll), continue writing your affirmations. Write them everywhere and any time you can and watch how you and others start to live this truth, practice it, soak yourself in this new reality you are creating.

These shifts are really, really cool to experience, especially as they start to happen.

Soundcheesy?? It totally is. And it totally works.

In order to move past mental blocks, you need to thoroughly and unconditionally forgive yourself. I don't care if you have led a hard life of crime or if you're a person with loads and loads of Victorian guilt; you need to step back and know, TRUST that self-forgiveness is the *only way to move on.*

Guilt is an absolutely wasted emotion. Sitting around and feeling guilty does nothing but add toxic elements your existence (not to mention your energy) and is beyond detrimental to your recovery and/or life improvement journey. Feel bad for maybe 2 seconds, but then ditch that guilt. Have a short-term memory about whatever it is you're feeling guilty about.

My favorite analogy for this would be a football player, more specifically a quarterback. Say he makes an egregious error like throwing an interception. His team is down several points and he has one more chance to throw a great pass and, hopefully, score a touchdown when the receiver catches the ball.

Does he sit around and wallow in shame about the interception he just threw? Absolutely not. What good what that do?

So what does he do? He regroups in a huddle with his team, explains the next play, revises his strategy for the team, and goes about executing his next pass. He does not dwell. He does not sit around and cry. He moves on. He moves himself and his team forward, figuratively (and hopefully literally too). He very likely even wins the game on this last play, despite the fact that he was under a boat-load of pressure. And the only reason he is able to do so is because he ditched his potential self-deprecating thoughts about the previous play and worked from a new, blank canvas.

Take Some You-Time

Once you have released your guilt, it is time to take the time for YOU that you need. It may sound unrealistic, depending on your circumstances, but taking the time to dream and let what you love about life soak in is absolutely necessary for welcoming improvements into your life.

Now, I realize we are busy. Time is scarce. We have obligations, families, events, social lives, work commitments, etc. Who has the time to sit around and dream, you may ask! Well....You do! It just takes a tiny bit of astuteness, intuition and a little efficiently appropriated time.

Yes, all you need to do to dream is to be present in your daily life. Practice being in the moment and then during each daily activity, ask yourself: Is this something I enjoy? Is this something I want to spend time on? Money on? Is this something I want more or less of in my life?

Assess these questions quickly – don't spend a lot of time on them – and then move on with your day. Notice at what points in your day you forget how fast or slow time is happening, or when you lose track of time altogether. What are you doing during these times? Are you working, playing tag with your kids, singing, telling jokes, walking your dog, spending time with friends? It all counts – and counts big.

Take these activities that you love and commit to spending more time doing them. No matter what it takes. I repeat: no matter what it takes. It may not happen overnight. It may not even happen in a period of a few months, but as time passes, continue to refresh your commitment to these activities, even if for five minutes a day.

Additionally, take a minute when you can to scribble on a post-it note or write in the notes app on your phone all the things you want to do more of in your life, the things that are worth the time and money to you.

The things you enjoy for pure pleasure. The things you deem important, essential, productive, satisfying. This is called prioritizing, and it will work wonders as you are carving out time for *you*.

YOU time is a huge part of writing your self-love-filled life story. (And again, even if you can't take that time in large quantities, make what you can do count. And count big.) If we don't take the time for ourselves, we will run on empty, sputter, and eventually run out of gas. This empty frenetic energy is what makes people miserable in life. It contributes to illness, leaves us overworked and underpaid. And definitely does not satiate our self-love palette that needs nourishment too.

When to Say "No" (*Just Say "No"*)

Yes, for us people pleasers it is hard to do. And when you're climbing up the corporate ladder or wanting to be an awesome soccer mom or trying to care for an elderly parent, it is especially hard. But here's the gist: do not over-commit. Say no to things that leave you overwrought and running on empty.

Saying no to things that aren't your responsibility is actually quite empowering! It leaves you some time and space and, for once, lets someone else pick up his/her slack (if he/she has been slacking). It helps others help *you*. Of course, you can return the favor sometime, but for now, saying no to excess obligations or even asking for a hand will give you so much more time and space to mentally and emotionally decompress and, in turn, nourish *your* spirit.

Embrace Patience and Trust the Process

Ah, patience. Be patient, my friend. These changes are not going to happen overnight. Success does not occur at a calculated, even, or strategically arranged pace. Success is often messy at first, so whatever you do, be patient. Your body / mind / spirit / may take some time to catch up with you. Have faith. The change will happen.

Every time you progress forward, a new challenge will present itself – this I can assure you. The saying goes, "new level, new devil", and it's right. Suddenly, when you are in a new, even freer, more evolved headspace you have fresh eyes. They are fresh and ready to go, but they are also new. So when a problem presents itself, you may have some awkward adolescent time trying to figure it out.

Whatever you do, though, keep going. You *will* figure it out; after some practice, you will even master it.

Chapter 2 The Best Mind Body Tools to Get and Stay Motivated

Now I'm going to tell you about my every-day morning routine, and I want you to take notes here. LOL, but really. Morning routines are incredibly important for setting your day up for success, and if you don't have one, now is the time to change that. Sleeping past your alarm, skipping a morning shower, and shoving down a Pop Tart for breakfast at the last traffic light you hit before you arrive at your office is just not going to cut it anymore.

Imagine, if you will, that you have an 8am work meeting. You set your alarm for 5:30am with intent on hitting the gym, cooking a light breakfast, taking a shower and driving to work. But you're tired, so you hit snooze, hit snooze again, then again. Before you know it, it's 7am, you've missed your time to work out, so you jump out of bed, hit the shower, grab a Power Bar and rush to get to work.

You are a little groggy still, flustered, and feeling guilty about not working out. You haven't taken the proper time for yourself to set up a fab day. And your energy around the office reflects it. This negative energy actually invites more negativity into your day. In fact, on this type of sub-par morning, I wouldn't be surprised if your boss came in and asked where you were at the 7:30am meeting you had totally forgotten about.

Setting yourself up for success in your day is the goal here, and skimping by on "doing just what you need to" is low frequency and asking for more drama. Now, imagine a morning where you wake up on the first buzz of your alarm. You tell yourself that today is going to be a wonderful day and that something, even if only one thing, great is going to happen today. You make your bed, brush your teeth, go for a quick run, shower, make a healthy smoothie for breakfast and allow yourself plenty of time to get dressed for work – and for some of you, even enough time to put on eye liner.

You arrive at the office, and your boss rushes into your office abound with compliments from a report you did last Tuesday. He presented it to his superiors, and they loved it. They even want to consider you for a position higher up in the company. I am not claiming it works as magically as this every time, but the universe works in mysterious and energy-related ways. So you might as well set yourself up for the latter.

Yes, there are those days where we just need an extra hour of sleep. But, really, that should not be the norm. Go to bed at a decent hour, so you can wake up pretty refreshed and ready to start the day...

The Power Hour (Inspired by Tony Robbins)

You really need to do the following: Reserve a "POWER HOUR" in the morning for yourself. (This may require that you set your alarm for a very early time, but know this will soon become a part of your morning routine that you will never ever want to forfeit. That's how valuable and life-changing this is.)

A Power Hour is a time for you to partake in a few small exercises that will change your days, one day at a time, and also change your life, over time. Remember... Life is not a dress rehearsal. We must do our best as often as possible, so no whining and commit to this for at least a week. Promise!

Experiment with these exercises. See how they affect you. Challenge yourself to make it happen. Then reward yourself with a nice healthy dinner out and a yoga class or massage at the end of the week (or whatever it is that you enjoy, at this stage of my life, I prefer to stick to healthy activities because they help me re-charge my batteries).

The Power of Journaling- How to Stay Motivated with Journaling (inspired by Julia Cameron)

*MORNING PAGES – These are time consuming, yes, so you may have to set your alarm for 30 minutes earlier or move something else (aka your workout) into a time slot later in the day in order to get the Morning Pages done. But, TRUST ME, they are BEYOND worth it.

What are Morning Pages, you ask? Well! Morning pages are a tool that will help you release anger, resentment, and guilt and help you celebrate your small successes and, in turn, help you build upon them to bring your dreams even closer into your reality.

Another name for "Morning Pages" is "Free Write". What that means is you have a notebook right beside your bed (it can be a cheap $1 notebook from the local drugstore for – or, of course, you can get a little spiffy and go the fancy, decorative route). When you wakeup, roll over, grab the notebook and start writing your three pages.

What should you write about? ANYTHING. EVERYTHING. Whatever comes to your mind, just say it on the page. Even if you think it is awful, bitter or just plain stupid, write it.

Write quickly and write whatever comes to your mind, even if it is "I don't want to do the laundry, my dog just peed on the carpet, I love my boyfriend", etc. Sometimes what you write will be mundane; other times it will be intelligent, witty, even brilliant. Some of my absolute *best* ideas have come from doing Morning Pages.

Another word for Morning Pages is called the "brain drain" because what this writing exercise allows us to do is to empty our brains of toxic, negative thoughts. Upon finishing the three pages, we leave the notebook by our bedside, our worries, ideas and joys behind and then go about our day feeling proactive, not to mention filled with more positive energy (as all the thought toxins have been released).

Note: I cannot take credit for this tool. The idea originally came from the brilliant Julia Cameron in her incredibly useful book "*The Artist's* Way". Shameless plug: go buy it and work through it. The Morning Pages and other tools from this book have been miracle workers for me. I cannot recommend it highly enough.

How to Use Affirmations to Get and Stay Motivated (how to brainwash yourself)

*AFFIRMATIONS: After your Morning Pages, save a little space (maybe half a page) to write some affirmations. (We talked about those earlier; I hope you remember!) Start taking things that you want to have more of in your life and include them in your affirmations. For example, if you want more money in your life, an affirmation such as, "Money flows towards me, and I am well-compensated for my efforts at work". If you want to tone up and feel stronger, you could say, "I am strong". If you want to get over your negative body image, try, "I am a beautiful beam of light no matter what".

Again, choose an affirmation that speaks to you – in a positive way, or even an affirmation to which you have a negative or uncomfortable reaction. (Sometimes a strong negative reaction towards an affirmation or area of weakness means we need to really work on that specific area. The best growth happens here.)

Write the affirmation over and over and over again. Maybe 10-20 times, following your Morning Pages. Choose one or two and stick with them for a few days. Stand back, and watch your energy – and your life priorities shift for the better. Behold, productive satisfaction will feel and *be* more within reach.

Meditation to Stay Motivated?

The third activity for your "Power Hour" is meditation. Now, *don't* let that word freak you out! Think: five minutes of quiet time, like in kindergarten. Sit somewhere in your room or in a room that brings your great joy. Sit cross-legged or in a way that's comfortable for you, and start to breathe slowly and deliberately. Focus on your breath. Breathe in and out, in and out. Picture the air going into your lungs, resting there for a second and then out.

When thoughts of the day ahead of you creep in, relax, let them seep out your pores and go back to focusing on your breath. In and out, in and out. Like a steady heartbeat. Take at least five minutes a day to do this.

I know what you're thinking…Meditation for motivation? Really?

After all, doesn't meditation have to do with just resting and being content? And if motivation is anything, it's the drive to achieve or gain something.

But meditation is about more than contentment and peace of mind. Meditation is about clarity and living in an honest, straightforward relation to your world. Meditation does not just make a permanent dent on your cushion. It also makes a deep impact on the way you live your life and how you get and stay motivated. Besides, things go better when you are at peace with yourself (here I refer to internal peace, you don't have to spend hours on meditation mats).

Your Power Hour- How to Get the Best of It and Stay Motivated Throughout the Day

I know it's hard to prioritize this time for yourself. See what you can do. Even if the meditation happens for five minutes before you go to bed, that works too. Do what works for you, but try to stick to the Morning Pages early in the morning. Those will really set your day up to be great.

Also, remember: Each and every one of these practices is, well....a *practice*. You can't run a marathon without training, just like you can't change your life or do a 180 on one aspect of your life overnight. You have to practice. Over time, the change will come.

Throughout my continued journey of self-development and growth, the lesson of long-term consistency has been the hardest thing to learn. Previously, I would do one day of these activities, not see a ton of change right away and then quit or, even worse, give up. Nope, nope. Doesn't work that way.

The trick is "slow and steady wins the race". And if that pace is not your forte (it's not mine, either), practice. Break these exercises down. No need to tackle the whole enchilada at once. Start your first week with just doing the Morning Pages a few times. See how you feel. Then add in the affirmations, then the meditation.

Pretty soon, you'll have an awesome morning routine that will keep you in the moment, present, and ready to take on life's challenges at their core. At your core. Because your core is strong and ready for the tasks at hand. You just have to prime it a bit.

Chapter 3 Your Vision for Life and (Vision Boards)

Okay, ready? This one is my favorite. It's called a vision board, and it, too, will change your life, *especially* if you are a visual person like myself. (And if you're not as visual, not to worry – it will still help you a ton.)

A vision board consists of images that portray your dream life. These images can be cut out from magazines, newspaper, printed from online – whatever. The only rule is the images must speak to you. They must evoke a powerful feeling of joy, satisfaction and even a little fear. (Even our best dreams can be scary!)

Plaster several images on a piece of poster board, preferably sparkly or a bright, fun color, and tape it to the wall. Put this vision board in your plain view, in a place where you can see it regularly. The bathroom mirror is an excellent place. Look at it often, revel in it, and ask yourself, *How am I going to make these visions come true?*

Once you have your vision board, look at each individual picture. Start with picture number one. Ask yourself, *by what time in my life you would I like to be living out the vision or goal that my item number one represents?*

Say it is a picture of a boat (it could be a small sail boat or a yacht – whatever (get ready…) floats your boat!).

Laughs aside, take a look at the boat picture and work backwards. Say in three years you would like to own a boat for you and your family, and you are nowhere near doing so. Think to yourself, what do I need to have a boat and when do I need to have it? If it's money, how will you earn, acquire, borrow and / or manifest it? Before money, maybe you realize that you are a bit of a workaholic, and you will need *time* to spend on that boat. How will you go about changing your life, so that more time becomes available to be with your family and enjoy your new boat?

Backing up even further, maybe the whole family-time / boat theme has gotten you thinking that you would like your two year-old to have a little brother or sister. Perhaps you think about some family planning and talk to your wife or husband about expanding your family to complete your vision.

Making your vision board opens up the world of possibilities to you and your dreams. In a way it is very much a blank canvas to paint your own reality. You may even find dreams that you didn't know you have. I did!

For the longest time, I have been afraid of heights and falling. It's a natural fear – many people have it, of course – but for me, it stops me from doing some fun things I know I would like to try.

One time, I was on an adventure camping trip, and the instructor told us we had to do a long (not to mention incredibly high-up) zip line at the end of a ropes course. I was terrified. My entire team of fellow campers went one by one down this zip line, no problem. I, of course, was last, and, unfortunately for me, the only way to get down from the ropes course was the zip line. In other words, I had to make the big jump.

My fellow camping-mates cheered me on and encouraged me to do it, to take the leap down the 125-150 foot drop. Well? It only took an hour, but I finally made the jump and slid down the zip line.

And you know what was incredibly crazy and awesome? I *loved* it. The thrill was exhilarating. Everyone cheered me on. Upon my landing, I was shaky from my previous fear of jumping and from my joy that I finally did something I didn't think I could do. Something I was deeply afraid of.

The point of this story is this: The zip line experience and my ultimate success at taking the leap helped me realize that I have a dream – something to go on my vision board – of going bungee jumping. Dropping from a really high surface and only being attached by an elastic cord.

And THIS from the girl who didn't want to jump off a zip line platform!

You see, vision boarding is about digging a little deeper and finding what experiences in your past you have loved. Vision boarding helps you envision these experiences play out to the n-th degree, so you can then put pieces of your life-puzzle together to make your goals happen in the truest and best version you can. All the dreams are there, waiting for you. You just have to narrow down life's many options and decide what it is that you want to go after.

And you have to make a plan.

Yes, now that we have *what* we want down on paper and a few details about *how* we are going to pursue these things, we need to set the exact timing for all of this to happen. Here's my suggestion, based on how I have manifested certain dreams and made them come true: Buy or make a calendar to fill out with the specific steps you need for your vision to be realized.

If you take the boat example, by what date do you need to have the money to purchase the boat? Then work backwards from there. In other words, what is the step you need to have completed in order to make the additional money? Is it that by a certain date you will pick up some extra work? Perhaps you will take out a loan by a certain date or ask to borrow the money from your rich aunt, who really loves and supports you in any way she can.

No matter what, get specific with the details of what you need to happen. Set a timeline. The universe is fond of specifics– and once you put these details and desires out into the universe and set a plan to go after these visions, watch the details and opportunities start to flow your way.

The final step to your vision board process is to, well, en*vision* what your dreams (and life) will be like once you have achieved them. In other words, what will your life look like once you have your boat? Will you be working less? More? Will you have another child in the picture or be working less (or more)?

Use your senses to really, really imagine what your life will be like with that boat. Smell the ocean, picture the look on your wife's face, or your children's faces, when you show them the new boat. Envision your own confidence level, as you will have created something incredible in your life that you truly wanted to come into fruition. You made it happen.

Envisioning these details is super important for your follow through and, as we said before, your intrinsic motivation level. Your dreams are most likely all inspired by intrinsic motivation. Your vision, your goals, too. So, in order to make them realized, pinpoint what it is about the items on your vision board that make you happy, satisfied, content and excited.

Then go out and get 'em.

Another note about vision boards: update them every month or few months. Our dreams and goals change as we go along. Our ideas evolve as we see certain elements of our visions begin to play out. Make sure your vision board corresponds to your current vision, not one you created last fall and have kind of forgotten about.

Also, stay super committed to checking in with your vision board. As our lives become busy and our priorities change throughout the year, as holidays and celebrations happen or as harder life events occur, keep checking in with your vision board. As said before, put it in a prominent place where you can see it often.

Follow these steps and behold, your vision will start to play out in numerous ways you heretofore never could have imagined. I cannot wait for you to try this! So, bust out some sparkly poster board, colored pens or pencils, your awesome imagination, and get to work.

What if you have no idea what to put on your vision board? Or what if you have so many ideas that you need to narrow them down?

Here are some suggestions:

Take a journey in your mind back to when you were a kid. After all, we all still have a kid inside us *somewhere*. So, access that inner child and reminisce about what you liked to do when you were younger. What made the time pass quickly over the summer vacation from school? What got you jazzed about your day? Was it sports, music, friendships, games, theatre, math class?

Whatever it was, think about how you could bring more elements of those desired activities into your daily life. Could you sign up for music lessons as an adult? Could you join a pick up basketball league or coach your son's soccer team? It all counts big time when it comes to making your vision board.

Another idea about how to figure out your dreams and visions is to imagine yourself at the end of your life. This one is a little harder, but definitely worth a try. Yes, at the end of your life, what would you like to have accomplished or seen played out in your lifetime that you would have liked to have been a part of? Use this exercise to influence what you want to put on your vision board.

Additionally, think about at the end of your life what you would have told your current self. For example, I can tend to be a bit of a worrier. *Am I doing it right, am I going to succeed?* I catch myself worrying about these things often.

In my older life, though, I imagine elderly-self telling my current self to *not worry*, but rather enjoy the ride a bit more. So then, I could incorporate elements of what it's like to enjoy life more into my vision and vision board.

This exercise will help you prioritize your vision-to-do list, as well. We only have so much time on this earth, much of it not to be taken for granted. So, what are the more important things – or things that are more important to *you* that you would like to achieve in the next few months, year, five years, etc.? And what can you let fall by the wayside?

I really hope you have an awesome time with your vision board. Give yourself permission to be a kid again for an evening and really imagine a new and improved life for yourself and/or your family. And enjoy!

Chapter 4 How to Turn Negative into Positive (How to Deal with Adversity)

Now for the hard part. We must take a look at a few negative aspects of change – but don't worry. They won't stay negative for long. See, as you change and grow and become even more fabulous in this process, you will very likely come up against a few obstacles (aka road blocks).

Here's how to deal with a few of the biggies:

How to Deal with People who Question Your Self-Improvements

When we grow, if others, specifically friends and family, remain static, they may not exactly love or appreciate the changes we are making. In fact, they may even try to slow us down or stop us from moving forward.

You see, sometimes people get so used to us being the way we have always been, even if that way is a bit "blocked", and as we liberate our own minds and spirits, it seems a bit scary for other people. As we grow and our visions of what is possible expand, we no longer fit into the mold that they are so used to seeing us in.

It will take some adjusting for them, too.

In most cases, our family and friends still love and care for us, so we need to be patient with their critiques and warnings. As we grow, they may fear we are "getting too big" or "acting weird" – metaphorically, of course – but what's really happening is that we are expanding our idea of the possibilities available to us and to those around us. Again, just understand where they are coming from.

Careful with Toxic People...

In a few instances, though, as our perspectives evolve for the better and more liberated us, some friends and family members emerge as, um, a little toxic. These are the toughies to deal with. Toxic friends and families can sabotage our efforts if we let them. And it's easy to let them.

As you make changes and self-improvements on your journey, watch out for the person in your life who suddenly becomes very needy with your time and attention. Perhaps they were always needy and you didn't realize it, or, perhaps, they are subconsciously noticing your changes and become a little scared.

Either way, assess to what degree these people still fit into your life. You may need to distance yourself from them for a while, and that is a-okay. Screen their calls a bit and call them back when you have a moment to yourself – on your watch. Or don't call them back at all. When you are about to do your Power Hour and they call you in a mini-crisis, don't answer your phone right away. Do what you need to do for *you*. You'll be much better prepared to handle the situation, anyway, after you've had time to do your Morning Pages and affirmations, etc.

Decide in what capacity it is ideal for you to have these "toxic" personalities in your life, and if you can't kick someone deserving to the curb immediately, decide in what capacity you can handle them *without* them interfering with your progress.

How to Deal with Self-Sabotage

Sabotage - Okay, this one is a BIGGIE, so be on the lookout anywhere and everywhere you think sabotage may be lurking.

When you are going along, making awesome changes in your life, and your dreams, visions and goals are being actualized, it's all good, right?!?!? Um....not exactly. See, what can happen, if we're not careful, is something called self-sabotage.

Self-sabotage is your mind's scared section that subconsciously tells you that growing and achieving your own greatness is scary, so you try to stop yourself, whether on purpose or not.

I like to use this example. For the longest time, whenever things would start to go well in my life, I would get sick. A cold, the flu, some random bladder infection, whatever. But no matter how I tried to change it, every time life got great, I would have to check out of the greatness for a week or two or three and my improvements would come to a screeching halt. (Yes, I know stuff happens and we all get sick, but this was a tad more psychological in nature.)

I would end up on these doctor visits, one after the other, thinking something was really wrong, and they would tell me it was simply a stubborn virus, which, in hindsight, was probably true.

The point here is that I'd learned this pattern of sabotage early in my life – for whatever reason – and that it was playing a large (too large) role in my adult life.

It had to go. So, I journaled (aka did my Morning Pages) and changed my affirmations to include statements about healthy bodies and minds. It took work, lots of work, actually, but I no longer get down the road of success and have to back up a few weeks just to take care of some grave ailment.

The point is this. Be on the lookout for self-sabotage. Especially as you get closer and closer to achieving some of the items on your vision board, keep a keen eye on your own efforts to subconsciously slay your progress.

And whatever you do, don't give into it. Additionally, we have other people's sabotage efforts to deal with. Remember those toxic friends? Yes, make sure they are not sabotaging you, either. They may even do it without realizing it.

Your Awareness is Your Responsibility

Again, be especially aware of when you get close to your visions and dreams. Or even when you get close to a benchmark on your journey toward them. A friend will likely have a crisis, or a family member may need you to babysit your niece when it's your last opportunity of the day to work on you and your goals.

I'm not saying ditch all responsibility here; but I am saying keep your eyes and ears aware that this will happen and be very thoughtful and purposeful about where you want to spend your time, energy, and efforts. Keep your eyes on the prize – because you absolutely deserve to. Don't jive so much with people who suck the life out of you or negative spirits who just bring you down.

In fact – and this is the next section – find the positive, high frequency spirits who lift you up and act as solid role models for where you want to be…

Your Hero: How to Get Inspired

So, now you're hanging out with the cool kids. The fun, high frequency go-getters and you suddenly develop a hero-crush on one. A "hero-crush" is someone you've pinpointed as an awesome role model. He / she is doing what *you* want to be doing and can give you lots of pointers on how to help get you where you want to be.

A hero-crush understands the necessity of having someone to look up to, as well as jive with on a neutral level (aka just hang out and let each other's energy bounce off themselves). A hero-crush could be older, younger, fatter, thinner, richer, poorer than you. It's just someone who "gets it", someone who is reaching for the stars and maybe has already landed on a few.

Surround yourself with these hero-crushes as often as possible. Emulate their behaviors, plant yourself in places where you might find them, and then make yourself and your aspirations known. This activity has done wonders for me, so I highly recommend it. So much of life and success involves networking and relationships based on awesome energy, so now is your chance – go out and find it!

Conclusion: Be Your Best Self

Here are my last words of advice: Be you. Be positively the best you that you can be. Do *not*, for any reason, settle. Life is short, and as stated before, is not a dress rehearsal. This is the real deal, yo. So pull yourself up by the bootstraps and set that alarm for 5 am. Think it's impossible? Not true; someone is doing it. And you should be too.

Never be afraid to ask for help. Whether you need to seek out a therapist or friend or hero-crush to help you seal the deal on success, do it. Asking for assistance is especially important when you are getting in your own way.

Think about TEAM YOU

The team of people behind you – your friends, family, pet, teachers, therapists, hero-crushes, etc. – should be excellent, and that is something you have absolute control over. For the most part, we control whom we interact with. We can elevate our frequency and push ourselves to be even better simply by working to surround ourselves with the best TEAM YOU possible.

It's a little bit like this: I had a therapist once who was criticized for driving a nice Lexus, as someone thought it was pretentious. Regarding this, this therapist made an excellent point: She said, "I am in charge of helping you work on your thoughts, emotions, ideas, and beliefs. My job is important. To society, yes, but more importantly, to you, the patient. Would you rather I drive a beat up Geo?"

I could not agree more. She was a part of my TEAM ME, and I most certainly wanted her driving a nice car because in an odd way, her car was a reflection of her success and, in turn, how well she would work with me to be *my* best. Boom!

Another word of advice: Stay the course. Be as consistent as you possibly can with the exercises in this eBook. Practice the Morning Pages, your Power Hour, meditation, yoga, even though it was not mentioned before. Get yourself in the absolute best headspace to go out and conquer your day. Each night tell yourself that something great is going to happen the next day. Because when you say this, it will.

When things don't go your way, take a step back and look at your overall arc. Are you still going in the direction you desire?

Continue to stay the course, even though once in a while it may need to be revised. Keep moving along your arc.

Prioritize inspiration (aka Brainwash Yourself)

Listen to inspirational audio books. Read books you have interest in. Go hear a guest speaker at a local college – or YouTube his or her speech. With the internet, the world (and an endless supply of inspiration) is at our fingertips, so take advantage as much as humanly possible.

Relax. I *know* this is easier said than done. But if you haven't taken a vacation in ten years, figure out how you can make that happen. And take *two* weeks if you can! Even if you can't, take a day or two off and create a mini creativity day in which you put together your vision board and brainstorm about the awesome steps you are about to take in your life.

Be Specific and Have Deadlines

Purchase or make a calendar that shows when you want to do what. Review this calendar super often. Revisit it daily, if at all possible – at the *very* least, weekly. Keep your vision fresh in your mind. Move what is important to the front burner, and keep it there. (Move the excess tasks and peripheral goals to the back burner).

Do Not Take Crap from Anyone

You will very likely receive some criticism about your moving forward and your awesome, perhaps new, motivation to better yourself. Other people – friends and family, in particular – may not agree with that vision. Remember: It is *your* vision and your vision only. It only affects others if you are disrespectful or manipulative towards them. Otherwise, it is their job to cheer you on.

At first, keep your vision quiet. When you are a tiny little vision-fledgling, the *last* thing you need is criticism from others. In fact, that could ruin your vision before you even get started. So keep quiet until you are further on your way and have some solid footing underneath you. Then walk the walk. If other people refuse to support you, that is not your concern.

Dream big. Go big or go home.

Yes, you may end up with several failures – I most certainly have – but it takes many tries until we figure out our success rhythm, how we maneuver ourselves and practice achieving.

Don't get caught up in "realistic".

Reality will win out if you let it, so think big. Think vast. Think tall and wide and deep and thoroughly. Know that you have the power to change someone's life and, most specifically, your own. Understand the value in that. And then go out and spread the love.

Stay in shape.

Yes, physical shape. There is nothing more empowering than a workout and nothing less empowering than feeling overweight, lazy or un-motivated. Keep your physical activity level as high as possible. Your older self and health will thank you, and it will give you one less thing to worry about as you age. Keep the standard high on this. Physical exercise has been known to release endorphins and feel-good chemicals in the brain. When we are setting ourselves up for success, we need all the feel-good-ness we can get!

Lastly, do not settle. If you want something, fight for it. If you get beaten the first time, do not – I repeat – do *not* give up. The universe responds to tenacity, and your confidence level will thank you. You will persevere if you keep going. Refresh your goals, yes, and stay very specific about them, but do what it takes to make the life you want to happen take place.

Keep high standards for yourself.

Practice the exercises provided. Keep your frequency high. Write, play music, learn a new language, ride a horse, volunteer at a local homeless shelter, take pictures of the sky and edit them until you love them. Laugh, giggle, double over as often as possible. Sing in the shower. And in public. Who cares!?!?!

We get one life. One. Get serious about changing it for the better. And then go out and do so. Bust your hump and make it rain goodness. Because you can, you deserve to, and the world is a much better place because you are the absolute fabulous you we need….

Final Words

If you enjoyed this book and found something to experiment with, try out, share or commit to we are delighted.

Health and happiness can be found through many avenues and for all of them the journey itself is usually the joy. The destination is what we want to achieve, but it is in getting there that we constantly find out more about ourselves and our own uniqueness. And this is the most fascinating of all.

Until we meet again in another book – be healthy, be happy, be beautiful inside and out.

Sending you lots of love from here,

Maya Faro

For similar books, visit:

www.YourWellnessBooks.com

www.LOAforSuccess.com

****

One more thing, before you go, could you please review this book online? It's you I am writing for and your feedback is very important to me. Thank You☺

www.ingramcontent.com/pod-product-compliance
Lightning Source LLC
Chambersburg PA
CBHW042120100526
44587CB00025B/4135